DINOSAUR WORLD

Hard-headed Dinosaurs

Robin Birch

CHELSEA CLUBHOUSE

An Imprint of Chelsea House Publishers
A Haights Cross Communications Company

Philadelphia

This edition first published in 2003 in the United States of America by Chelsea Clubhouse, a division of Chelsea House Publishers and a subsidiary of Haights Cross Communications.

Chelsea Clubhouse
1974 Sproul Road, Suite 400
Broomall, PA 19008-0914

The Chelsea House world wide web address is www.chelseahouse.com

Library of Congress Cataloging-in-Publication Data

Birch, Robin.
    Hard-headed dinosaurs / by Robin Birch.
        p. cm. — (Dinosaur world)

    Includes index.
    Summary: Describes the appearance, eating habits, and habitat of hard-headed dinosaurs, including Pachycephalosaurus, Psittacosaurus, Triceratops, Styracosaurus, and Pachyrhinosaurus.

    ISBN 0-7910-7051-4
    1. Ornithischia—Juvenile literature. [1. Ornithischians. 2. Dinosaurs.] I. Title. II. Series.
    QE862.O65 B574 2003
    567.914—dc21

                                                                                    2002000843

First published in 2002 by
MACMILLAN EDUCATION AUSTRALIA PTY LTD
627 Chapel Street, South Yarra, Australia, 3141

Copyright © Robin Birch 2002
Copyright in photographs © individual photographers as credited

Edited by Angelique Campbell-Muir
Illustrations by Nina Sanadze
Page layout by Nina Sanadze

Printed in China

Acknowledgements
Department of Library Services, American Museum of Natural History (neg. no. PK51), p. 9; Auscape/John Cancalosi, p. 5, Auscape/Francois Gohier, p. 8 (top), Auscape/Ferrero-Labat, p. 25; Museum Victoria, p. 8 (bottom); © The Natural History Museum, London, p. 17; Getty Images/Photodisc, p.16 (left); Prehistoric Animal Structures, Inc., p. 16 (right); Royal Tyrrell Museum of Palaeontology/Alberta Community Development, pp. 21, 29.

While every care has been taken to trace and acknowledge copyright, the publisher tenders their apologies for any accidental infringement where copyright has proved untraceable.

Contents

Dinosaurs

Dinosaurs lived millions of years ago.
Some dinosaurs were huge and others
were quite small.

Many dinosaur bones became buried in the ground. Some turned into rock. Scientists dig up and study these **fossils**.

Hard Heads

Hard bone covered the heads of some dinosaurs. These hard-headed dinosaurs ate plants.

Some of these dinosaurs had heads like **helmets**. Others had **horns**, spikes, or big **frills** made of bone on their heads.

7

The hard-headed dinosaurs had beaks for breaking off plants. They had sharp teeth in their cheeks for cutting up the plants to eat. Their **skulls** show these hard beaks.

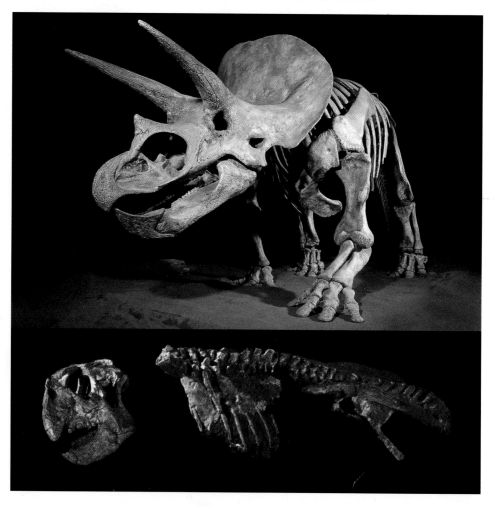

Hard-headed dinosaurs laid eggs, as all other dinosaurs did. Some eggs did not hatch. Over time they turned into rocks. Scientists have dug up many dinosaur egg fossils.

Pachycephalosaurus

(pak-ee-SEF-uh-lo-SAWR-ruhs)

Pachycephalosaurus was not a very big dinosaur. It stood 8 feet (2.4 meters) tall and measured up to 15 feet (4.5 meters) long. Pachycephalosaurus walked on two legs and had a **stiff**, heavy tail.

Pachycephalosaurus was a dome-headed dinosaur. Very thick bone almost 10 inches (25 centimeters) thick covered the top of its head. Small bony spikes and bumps surrounded the dome.

Some scientists think the dinosaurs crashed their heads together to fight. Other scientists believe Pachycephalosaurus butted the sides of other animals with its head.

Pachycephalosaurus had small, sharp teeth in its cheeks. It probably used these teeth to grind soft leaves, fruits, and seeds for food.

Psittacosaurus

(SIT-uh-ko-SAWR-uhs)

Psittacosaurus was a small dinosaur about 4 feet (1 meter) tall. It had a short, boxy head with extra bone at the back. Small horns stuck out of its cheeks.

Psittacosaurus walked and ran on two legs.
Its arms were much shorter than its legs.

Psittacosaurus had a sharp beak similar to a parrot's beak. Psittacosaurus probably used its beak to slice through nuts and other hard plant food. Psittacosaurus also had sharp cheek teeth for cutting up its food.

Psittacosaurus swallowed stones, as many other dinosaurs did. The stones stayed in its stomach to help mash up food.

17

Triceratops

(try-SAIR-uh-tops)

Triceratops was as heavy as an elephant. It had three horns on its face and a frill of bone at the back of its head.

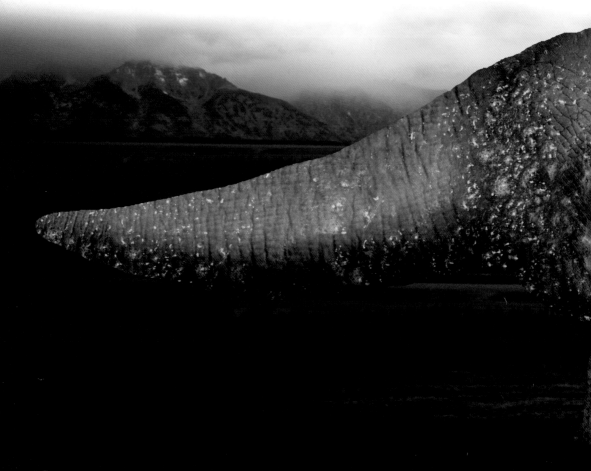

Triceratops walked on four strong legs. It had very thick, tough skin. Its large skull was up to 10 feet (3 meters) long.

Triceratops lived in large **herds**. The herds moved through **woodlands** looking for food. Triceratops used its beak to snip off twigs and leaves to eat.

Scientists have dug up many Triceratops bones and studied them. They have put the bones together to make **skeletons**.

Styracosaurus

(stih-RAK-uh-SAWR-uhs)

Styracosaurus had a **bulky** body, a thick tail, and a large head. It walked on four short legs. Styracosaurus had a horn on its nose that was nearly 2 feet (.6 meters) long.

At the back of its head, Styracosaurus had a frill with six long spikes along the edge. Skin covered the frill.

The frill and spikes protected Styracosaurus from meat-eating dinosaurs. Some scientists think Styracosaurus **charged** at these **predators**.

Styracosaurus lived in huge herds, probably in woodlands. The herds walked long distances in search of food. Many animals live in herds today.

Pachyrhinosaurus

(PAK-ee-rye-no-SAWR-uhs)

Pachyrhinosaurus stood 11 feet (3.5 meters) tall and measured 23 feet (7 meters) long. It had a beak like a parrot's beak to break off palm leaves and other plants to eat.

Pachyrhinosaurus had a large bump of bone on its face. This bone may have been a different shape on males and females. A short frill with two spikes sat at the back of its head.

Males may have fought by crashing the bones on their heads together. They also may have charged at predators to defend themselves.

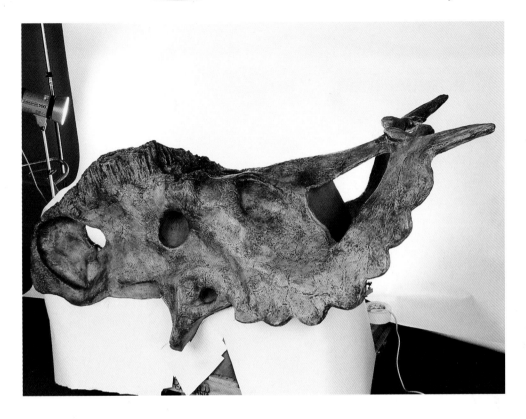

Scientists have often discovered many
Pachyrhinosaurus skeletons together in one
place. From these finds, they learned that
Pachyrhinosaurus lived in very large herds.

Names and Their Meanings

"Dinosaur" means "terrible lizard."

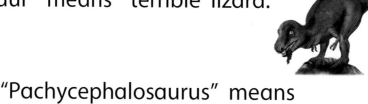

"Pachycephalosaurus" means "thick-headed lizard."

"Psittacosaurus" means "parrot lizard."

"Triceratops" means "three-horned face."

"Styracosaurus" means "spiked lizard."

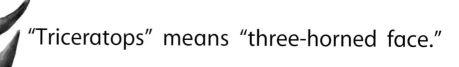

"Pachyrhinosaurus" means "thick-nosed lizard."

Glossary

bulky	to be large and take up a lot of space
charge	to rush forward in order to attack
fossil	something left behind by a plant or animal that has been preserved in the earth; examples are dinosaur bones and footprints.
frill	a bony shield on an animal's neck or at the back of the head; frills can be many shapes and sizes.
helmet	a hard covering that protects the head
herd	a large group of animals that live together
horn	a hard, bony growth on the head of an animal; many horns are pointed.
predator	an animal that hunts other animals for food
skeleton	the bones that support and protect an animal's body
skull	the bones of the head
stiff	does not bend
woodland	land covered mainly by trees

Index